NINJUTSU

Mastering the Martial Arts Series

Judo: Winning Ways

Jujutsu: Winning Ways

Karate: Winning Ways

Kickboxing: Winning Ways

Kung Fu: Winning Ways

Martial Arts for Athletic Conditioning: Winning Ways

Martial Arts for Children: Winning Ways

Martial Arts for Women: Winning Ways

Ninjutsu: Winning Ways

Taekwondo: Winning Ways

NINJUTSU

ERIC CHALINE

Series Consultant
Adam James
10th Level Instructor
Founder: Rainbow Warrior Martial Arts
Director: Natl. College of Exercise Professionals

MASON CREST
www.masoncrest.com

Mason Crest Publishers Inc.
450 Parkway Drive, Suite D
Broomall, PA 19008
www.masoncrest.com

Library of Congress Cataloging-in-Publication Data on file at the Library of Congress and with the publisher

Series ISBN: 978-1-4222-3235-4
Hardback ISBN :978-1-4222-3244-6
EBook ISBN: 978-1-4222-8673-9

First Edition: September 2005

Produced in association with Shoreline Publishing Group LLC

Printed and bound in the United States

IMPORTANT NOTICE

The techniques and information described in this publication are for use in dire circumstances only where the safety of the individual is at risk. Accordingly, the publisher copyright owner cannot accept any responsibility for any prosecution or proceedings brought or instituted against any person or body as a result of the use or misuse of the techniques and information within.

Picture Credits
Paul Clifton: 30.
Dreamstime.com: Nkrikvo 8; Fenriswolf 16; Davidstudio2008 29; Joeygil: 58.
Mary Evans Picture Library: 12, 18, 22.
Nathan Johnson: 6, 11, 15, 26, 35, 40, 43, 50, 53, 56, 64, 72, 75, 76, 85, 89.
Bob Willingham: 25, 38.

Front cover image: Stace Sanchez/KickPics

CONTENTS

Words to Understand: These words with their easy-to-understand definitions will increase the reader's understanding of the text, while building vocabulary skills.

Sidebars: This boxed material within the main text allows readers to build knowledge, gain insights, explore possibilities, and broaden their perspectives by weaving together additional information to provide realistic and holistic perspectives.

Heroic secret agent, Japanese Robin Hood, or merciless paid assassin—the ninja have several faces in the popular imagination.

INTRODUCTION

The journey of a thousand miles begins with a single step, and the journey of a martial artist begins with a single thought—the decision to learn and train. The Martial Arts involve mental and emotional development, not just physical training, and therefore you can start your journey by reading and studying books. At the very beginning, you must decide which Martial Art is right for you, and reading these books will give you a full perspective and open this world up to you. If you are already a martial artist, books can elevate your training to new levels by revealing techniques and aspects of history and pioneers that you might not have known about.

The Mastering the Martial Arts series will provide you with insights into the world of the most well-known martial arts along with several unique training categories. It will introduce you to the key pioneers of the martial arts and the leaders of the next generation. Martial Arts have been around for thousands of years in all of the cultures of the world. However, until recently, the techniques, philosophies, and training methods were considered valuable secretes and seldom revealed. With the globalization of the world, we now openly share the information and we are achieving new levels of knowledge and wisdom. I highly recommend these books to begin your journey or to discover new aspects of your own training.

Be well.
Adam James

 WORDS TO UNDERSTAND

ascetic Someone who practices strict self-denial as a means of self-discipline

daimyo Semi-independent feudal lords who ruled Japanese provinces from 1185 to 1867

exile Expulsion from a person's native country

feudal A social and political system in which peasants work for a powerful landowner in exchange for food and protection

fiefdom A piece of land held under the feudal system

kana Any of various Japanese syllabic alphabets

kanji Chinese characters

ruse A lie; a trick

Shinto Native religion of Japan, which stresses the holiness of natural objects

shogun Military rulers of Japan from 1185 to 1867

WHAT IS NINJUTSU?

Creeping out of the shadows of history, the ninja peers at us from behind his or her trademark black face scarf that obscures everything but his or her eyes. Part hero, part villain, the ninja was Japan's very own superhero.

Trained from childhood in the arts of war and deception, ninjas were at the height of their power during Japan's **feudal** age, from the 12th to the 17th centuries. The ninja's art, called ninjutsu, was not a single set of fighting techniques, like the modern Japanese martial arts of karate or judo. Rather, it was a composite made up of both armed and unarmed fighting methods drawn from native Japanese and Chinese traditions, as well as the "art of invisibility," the techniques and **ruses** the ninja developed in order to avoid detection.

WHAT'S IN A NAME?

The Japanese language is extremely rich and subtle in levels of meaning, much of which is lost in translation. The subtlety occurs not only in the spoken language, with its elaborate levels of politeness, but also in the way it is written. Japanese is written by combining three different systems: the 20,000 or so **kanji** (pictographic characters) borrowed from China, each of which stands for a whole word; and two syllabic alphabets, or **kana**, which are used to write word endings and foreign words. The choice of how a word is written in Japanese reveals much more than it would when written in our own simple, Roman alphabet.

The kanji "nin" means hidden, stealth, or secret; and the kanji "jutsu" means technique, or art. Thus, the literal translation of ninjutsu is "the technique (or art) of stealth." Most of Japan's martial arts now describe themselves as do, or "ways"; for example, aikido (the way of harmony) and kendo (the way of the sword). This description indicates that practitioners have chosen not just the study of a fighting technique, but also to follow a path that will guide their entire lives. The choice of the kanji "jutsu" indicates a much more practical approach, suggesting that ninjutsu is just a set of techniques to be learned and not a philosophy by which to live. Similarly, whereas Japanese martial artists describe themselves as ka (as in judo-ka or karatedo-ka), which indicates a vocation (as in gak-ka, which means "fine-arts painter"), the practitioners of ninjutsu are called "ninja," which incorporates the kanji "ja", meaning merely "person." While today, some ninjutsu schools prefer to call their art ninpo, meaning "the way of secrecy," this is a recent development that merely mimics the naming of the other well-established Japanese martial arts.

THE HOLLYWOOD NINJA

In the past three decades, the West has discovered a passion for the Asian martial arts, including ninjutsu and its mysterious practitioners, the ninja. The fruits of this interest have sometimes been bizarre, such

The ninja were not superhuman beings of legend, descended from demons, but rather, superbly trained professionals whose lives were dedicated to the mastery of their art.

A historical print of ancient Japan, with Mount Fuji visible in the distance. The heyday of the ninja clans was the feudal age, from the 12th to the 17th century, when Japan was ruled by a succession of military dictators, or shoguns.

as the comic book characters known as the "Teenage Mutant Ninja Turtles." In Hollywood films, the ninja themselves are portrayed either as cold-blooded assassins who assail the good guys (and who, despite their terrifying skills, are always defeated) or as Asian Robin Hoods fighting for truth, justice, and the Japanese way. In fact, the historical ninja were an intriguing mixture of good and bad, sometimes on the side of the forces of law and order, and sometimes at odds with them.

MYTHS AND HISTORY OF THE NINJA

Japan is a country where historical fact and myth are still intertwined in complex ways. Take the imperial family, for example. Although the emperor has been the constitutional monarch since Japan's defeat by the United States and her allies in the Second World War (1939–1945), he is still believed by many older Japanese to be a direct descendant in an unbroken line stretching back to the sun goddess, Amaterasu-o-Mikami. The historical fact, however, is that the imperial succession has been broken several times and "helped along" several times more. In Japan, historical accuracy and "truth" are not always one and the same.

The origins of Japan's ninja clans are similarly obscured by legend. Some ninjutsu traditions claim that the ninja are descended from the storm god Susanoo and his creations: the half-crow, half-human demons called the tengu. The tengu had distinctively long noses, reminiscent of beaks, and were either red or black in color. They lived in the depths of the most remote forests and had supernatural powers, including the ability to fly, change their shape, and become invisible by wearing magical cloaks made of leaves. Like the other supernatural creatures of Japan, they sometimes helped and befriended humans who strayed into their realm; but sometimes they hindered them.

The ninja themselves spread legends of their supernatural origins. These stories had their uses. They served to awe and frighten the ninja's foes, and were also no doubt useful in discouraging the curiosity of any superstitious peasant who might be tempted to spy on the ninja villages and training camps.

THE CHINESE CONNECTION

In the sixth century A.D., a process of cultural importation from Korea and China came to fruition with the establishment of an imperial government in western Japan, complete with a capital city and a civil bureaucracy, under the leadership of Prince Shotoku (A.D. 574–622). The mainland culture that the Japanese adopted included the Chinese writing system (kanji), as well as the Buddhist religion. However, the introduction of a strange religion immediately caused friction with the priests and followers of the native **Shinto** faith, leading to a struggle that endured for the next two centuries.

Along with political institutions and religion, the Japanese imported other aspects of Chinese culture, including the martial arts and classic Chinese military texts, such as Suntzu's *Art of War* (c. 400 B.C.). This military manual describes two types of war: the tactics of battle and open warfare, and what would now be called "covert" operations, agitation, and espionage. It is likely that the ninja families obtained copies of the *Art of War* and used it as the basis for their operations.

Another version of ninja origins claims that they learned their techniques from **exiles** escaping from the collapse of China's T'ang Dynasty (A.D. 618–906). These escapees hid in the mountains south of Kyoto, where they passed on their secrets to the yamabushi, mountain warrior-**ascetics** who practiced an occult form of Buddhism called Mikkyo (or Shugendo).

With as many as 50 ninja clans, it is highly unlikely that there is a single explanation for the emergence of ninjutsu. Some ninja may have been the descendants of yamabushi or of Chinese exiles; while others were probably samurai who had lost their status after their lords had been defeated in battle, and they themselves had become **ronin**

Right: The ninja's trademark black outfit and fearsome arsenal of weapons, which seems so exotic to us today, was developed in feudal Japan. Many of the ninja's weapons were the agricultural implements of the day.

(masterless samurai). All that can be said with any certainty is that the traditions that became known as ninjutsu emerged in western Japan in the provinces of Iga (now the Mie prefecture) and Koga (now the Shiga prefecture) between the 7th and 12th centuries.

THE GOLDEN AGE OF NINJUTSU

In 1192, the emperor lost effective control of the government to a military dictator known as the shogun. The shogun was the head of the most powerful samurai clan. This became the pattern of government: a powerless figurehead emperor reigned in Kyoto, while the shogun actually ruled the people. This pattern lasted for the next 675 years.

In the feudal age, the weapon of choice was the katana, the samurai's long sword, which many ninja techniques and weapons were designed to combat.

The first **shogun** dynasty ruled from Kamakura, a city 31 miles (50 km) south of modern-day Tokyo, in eastern Japan. The Kamakura shoguns ruled for 138 years, and then they were themselves overthrown by a more powerful family. This jockeying for position among powerful feudal lords, or **daimyo**, created the perfect climate for the ninja families to operate in. The provinces of Iga and Koga were independent **fiefdoms** run by the ninja clans. Koga had as many as 50 ninja families, with 40 to 50 members each. Three great clans ruled Iga: the Hattori, the Momochi, and the Fujibayashi, the largest of which could call on the services of over 1,000 members. In their heyday, there were 25 ninja schools in Japan.

During the periods when the shoguns (the most powerful feudal lords of the time) were strong, they employed the ninja as spies and assassins, working covertly against one another. But in 1467, Japan entered a century of civil war, with all of the powerful feudal lords vying to become the next shogun. Open warfare gave the ninja even greater scope and influence. Although they occasionally took part in military operations with regular troops, the ninja were usually commandos or guerrillas, harassing the enemy, cutting his supplies and communications lines, spreading false rumors, and assassinating enemy generals.

THE LAST BATTLE

In 1568, the situation changed dramatically for the ninja with the emergence of the first of three great leaders, whose work would eventually lead to the unification of Japan. This first man was the brilliant but violent Oda Nobunaga (1534–1582). Succeeding to the leadership of his clan at the age of 17, he quickly established himself as

The samurai lords, or daimyo, employed the ninja, but the two groups never fully trusted one another. In the end, the samurai clans went to war to destroy the ninja.

the leading tactician of his day. Aided by his faithfull general, Toyotomi Hideyoshi (1537–1598) and his ally, Tokugawa Ieyasu (1543–1616), he overthrew the last shogun and began a military campaign to unite the country under his rule. Nobunaga would not tolerate opposition, and so when the Buddhist warrior-monks of Mount Hiei, near Kyoto, refused to submit to him, he attacked their strongholds and slaughtered them by the thousands.

Nobunaga then turned his gaze southward, to the ninja of the province of Iga, who were followers of Mikkyo Buddhism and had links with Nobunaga's enemies. Legend has it that he began to dislike this province when he fell from his horse while riding there, but he probably had better political reasons for fearing the ninja.

For one thing, they were too independent for his liking. Determined to conquer the whole of Japan, he reasoned that it would be foolish to leave so dangerous a force in his own backyard. In 1579, he sent one of his sons, Katsuyori, along with an army, to bring the province into submission. The ninja, who were brilliantly led, defeated the army and forced it to withdraw.

Furious, Nobunaga personally led a force of 40,000 men, outnumbering his enemy 10 to 1, into the province, where he inflicted a terrible revenge on the ninja for his son's defeat. On November 3, 1581, the largest ninja army ever assembled was defeated, and any ninja who could be found—man, woman, or child—was put to the sword.

Although beaten, the ninja were not finished. They still had a crucial role to play in the history of the unification of Japan.

THE SHOGUN'S MEN

In 1582, Nobunaga was ambushed in a temple by one of his own generals. To avoid capture, Nobunaga was forced to commit ritual suicide (called seppuku) by cutting open his own stomach. His principal ally, the young lord Tokugawa Ieyasu, was trapped in Osaka by Nobunaga's murderer and was forced to flee for his life. His only escape route eastward back to his castle at Okazaki (now called Nagoya and located in central Japan) lay through the provinces of Iga and Koga.

The Hattori ninja, who lived in the province of Iga, put aside their enmity for the Oda and agreed to help Ieyasu escape. Had they not done so, the whole course of Japanese history would have been changed. Together, Ieyasu and Nobunag's loyal general, Toyotomi Hideyoshi, defeated the traitor.

After the victory, it was General Hideyoshi's turn to attempt the unification of Japan. While on the surface Hideyoshi and Ieyasu were friends, there was a growing tension between them. Nevertheless, their alliance survived until Hideyoshi's death in 1598. Hideyoshi left a child heir as his successor. Taking advantage of the situation, Ieyasu quickly made his move. He defeated what had been Hideyoshi's army at the Battle of Sekigahara in 1600 and effectively became the undisputed ruler of Japan. Ieyasu was the first Tokugawa shogun, and his dynasty would rule the country for the next 268 years.

A grateful Ieyasu appointed the Hattori ninja to be his personal guards, giving them the cover of being gardeners in the castle of his new capital, Edo (now called Tokyo), in eastern Japan. The early years of Ieyasu's rule were troubled, with many revolts and challenges from rival lords, who themselves employed ninja assassins and spies. Ieyasu

NINJA DRESS AND WEAPONRY

Dressed all in black, the ninja's clothing was designed for covert missions. The ninja's arsenal contained many chain weapons (such as the one shown) that could be used to snag an opponent's hand or sword.

The last official action of the ninja agents of the Japanese government was to spy on the "Black Ships," the American warships that forced Japan to open its doors to the outside world in 1848.

survived several assassination attempts and, as a result, became wary of the power of the ninja clans. Aside from those that trained men in his own service, he banned all other ninja schools.

Deprived of their leaders and livelihoods, the former ninja became outlaws. They were now pursued by the officially recognized ninja, who were the shogun's policemen and spies. In the centuries of peace that followed, the shogun's ninjas were instructed to use their skills to police the great cities of Edo and Osaka.

But as early as the 17th century, the end was in sight for the ninja. War had not destroyed them, but two centuries of peace would sap their strength and almost extinguish them. Japan had been pacified, and the feudal lords no longer plotted to overthrow the shogun. In 1637, however, the ninja were called upon to serve the shogun in wartime one final time.

In 1614, the shogunate, fearing foreign domination, effectively sealed off Japan from the outside world, forbidding all foreigners from entering the country, and banning Christianity. The large community of Japanese Christians in the Nagasaki region rebelled in 1636, and the shogun sent an army to quell the rebellion. A group of 10 ninja, many of them old men by that time, were brought out of retirement and sent to spy for the government. Although they scored some minor successes, these old ninja failed to infiltrate the enemy stronghold primarily because they could not speak the Nagasaki dialect.

The very last action of the official Tokugawa ninja was in 1853, when a squadron of "Black Ships" under the command of the American Commodore Matthew Perry arrived in Japan to force the shogun to open the country to the outside world. ("Black Ship" was the Japanese name given to the American warships that arrived to force Japan to end its self-imposed isolation.) A ninja managed to get on board one of Perry's ships to spy on the foreign intruders, and stole two letters. Unfortunately, the letters held little of interest.

Fifteen years after Commodore Perry's historic visit, an alliance of feudal lords and reformers overthrew the Tokugawa shogunate, which was replaced by a reforming government under the nominal overlordship of the emperor. As Japan hastened to modernize its industries and army, the official ninja schools were closed down. During the next century, few in Japan had any interest in the ancient art of ninjutsu, and only a few of the original ninja families kept the traditions alive.

MODERN TIMES

For a few years, Japan's defeat in the Second World War in 1945 seemed to signal the death of its martial arts traditions. Seen as encouraging imperialism and militarism, the martial arts were, for a time, banned by the U.S. occupation authorities. The Japanese themselves saw little value in the ancient skills of the ninja, who by now were little more than folktale characters.

The renewal of interest in ninjutsu and the ninja began with the GIs returning to the U.S. after the war with ancient weapons and tales of "shadow warriors" with supernatural abilities. The ninja caught the imagination of the Japanese film and television industries, and soon, the imagination of Hollywood as well. The 1970s witnessed a craze for the martial arts of China and Japan, spearheaded by the movies of Bruce Lee. The ninja in his black facemask quickly became an immediately recognizable character in martial arts films.

While interest in the fictional ninja was picking up, American martial arts historians and martial artists were making a more serious investigation of ninjutsu. These people traveled to Japan to discover all they could about the ninja and their techniques. A few of them finally managed to contact the remaining ninja families, who reluctantly agreed to take them on as pupils. As a result, ninjutsu is now taught all over the world.

Two modern-day ninjutsu enthusiasts train in combat techniques. The renaissance of ninja techniques is largely due to interest in the East Asian martial arts of U.S. military personnel returning from the Pacific area and the U.S. occupation of Japan after the Second World War.

 WORDS TO UNDERSTAND

courtesan A female courtier or prostitute

halberd A combined spear and battle-ax

hierarchy A system in which grades of status or authority are ranked above each other

kunoichi Female ninja agent

paddy A field where rice is grown

taijitsu Literally, "body art," unarmed fighting techniques; these were based on Japan's own jujutsu

TRAINING TO BE A NINJA

Step back 700 years, to the year 1300. Japan, under the nominal control of the shogun in Kamakura, Is In chaos. The feudal lords who head Japan's samurai clans rule their provinces with little regard for the shogun, and even less for the powerless emperor, who is a virtual prisoner in his palace in Kyoto. They plot and form alliances and fight with the shogun's government and with one another—all with the help of ninja spies and assassins. The ninja clans themselves have grown quite powerful. No one dares to enter the provinces of Iga and Koga, where the ninja clans live, without their permission.

In those days, Japan was not a hospitable country; it had few natural resources, little land fit for cultivation, and the bulk of its terrain was mountainous and forested. While today Japan enjoys the benefits of a modern infrastructure of railways and roads, in the early 14th century, travel to many regions was dangerous and time-consuming. One such region was the province of Iga on the Kii Peninsula, south of the imperial capital, Kyoto.

A ninja launches a sword attack in the forest. The ninja traded on myths about their supernatural powers, but their real secret was the intensity and scope of their training in the fighting arts and psychological warfare.

The mountains of Iga are thickly forested. During the summer rains, the few roads and tracks are mired in mud or washed away altogether; in winter, snow falls so heavily that it cuts off the area for weeks. The land is poor and unyielding. If you were to travel up along the narrow, sheltered valleys in the mountains, you would come across isolated peasant villages. Unless you looked closely, you might not see any differences between these villages and others similar to them in other regions of Japan. They all seem to consist of small clusters of thatched farmhouses around a few fields, vegetable gardens, and **paddies**, with a small Buddhist temple and the red gate of a Shinto shrine.

But if you happened to be a little more observant, you might notice things indicating that this simple peasant village has some secrets. Maybe the headman's house is a little larger and better appointed than it should be; maybe the blacksmith is busier than if he were making only farm implements; maybe the inhabitants look a bit too well fed and dressed, and maybe they walk with more confidence and defiance than lowly peasants should. The villagers chat to you and offer you food and water, but something in their manner makes it plain that you are not entirely welcome, and that you should think about moving on while there is still time to reach the lowlands. You thank them for their hospitality and hurry away.

NINJA TRAINING

Let us imagine that two children, a boy named Ichiro and his younger sister, Okoi, live in an isolated village in Iga. Like Japanese children today, they have been spoiled by their parents and adult relatives, who allow them to get away with some very unruly behavior. Whatever they

The ninja shrouded their secrets in the religious rituals and languages of the Mikkyo sect of esoteric Buddhism, which they had learned from the yamabushi mountain warrior-ascetics.

Peter King, an 11th dan togakure ryu ninjutsu instructor, re-creates an outdoor ninja-training session in armed and unarmed fighting skills.

do, they are never scolded, and are always given treats.

Shielded by their own innocence and by the indulgence of their elders, they have never questioned why their father and elder siblings sometimes go away for months at a time and sometimes return injured. They have not wondered about the people who come and go from their house at night, why their house has hidden compartments and passageways, and why there are secret rooms full of hidden weapons and other mysterious devices. Now that the boy has turned six and his younger sister is five, however, their lives are about to change forever, for Ichiro and Okoi have been born into a ninja family, and whether they want to or not, they will be trained as ninja themselves.

BASIC TRAINING

Their training begins early with types of fitness exercises that we would recognize today. The ninja develop their stamina by going on grueling 50-mile (80-km) runs on the mountain paths around their villages. This early training will serve them well in later life, when they will be able to travel great distances without tiring and arrive more quickly than the enemy has anticipated. They increase their strength and muscular endurance by climbing trees and hanging from their branches, as well as from ropes, for long periods of time. They will require these skills when infiltrating castles or when hanging motionless under the eaves and ceiling spaces of a house while spying or awaiting an opportunity to strike.

Balance skills are taught by performing walking, running, and jumping exercises on a narrow tree trunk hewn of its branches to resemble a gymnast's high beam, as well as on tightropes. A good sense of balance is essential, as the ninja will often enter and leave a building across its roof. Swimming is also on the curriculum, as many Japanese castles and mansions have moats that must be swum across, or garden ponds and ornamental lakes that may serve as convenient hiding places. The ninja also practice breathing techniques that will allow them to stay underwater for long periods of time.

Another skill that is taught to the fledgling ninja is how to dislocate their joints by stretching, allowing them to reconfigure their bodies at will. This will serve several purposes during their operational lives. It will allow them to fit into spaces considered too small or awkward for an untrained human being; resist joint locks applied by their opponents in hand-to-hand combat; and, if captured, change their body shape, slip out of their bonds, and escape.

SPECIALIST SKILLS

Once finished with their basic training, Ichiro and Okoi will begin their studies in the specialist areas of ninjutsu. These studies vary from family to family and from school to school. Some families specialize in certain classes of weapons, while others specialize in styles of unarmed combat. However, there are common areas that all ninja study. These areas include **taijutsu** (unarmed combat); weapons training, including fighting using the bo staff, blade weapons hidden weapons, and chain and rope weapons; "the art of invisibility" (the art of hiding oneself); espionage; reconnaissance; psychological warfare; mapmaking and reading; and how to survive in the woods.

It is only when Ichiro and Okoi reach puberty that their training will diverge. Women in 14th-century Japan have a secondary place to men, but that does not mean they have no role to play at all. Japanese women are not kept locked away in harems. Samurai women are expected to follow the same honor codes as their husbands and to fight to the death, if necessary, for their lord and clan. They are trained in naginatajutsu (the art of the **halberd**) rather than kenjutsu (the art of the sword), because the halberd's longer reach gives them an advantage over a swordsman.

Moreover, when a girl grows to maturity, from then on in, her training will exploit the opportunities a woman might have to get close to a male

HAND-TO-HAND COMBAT

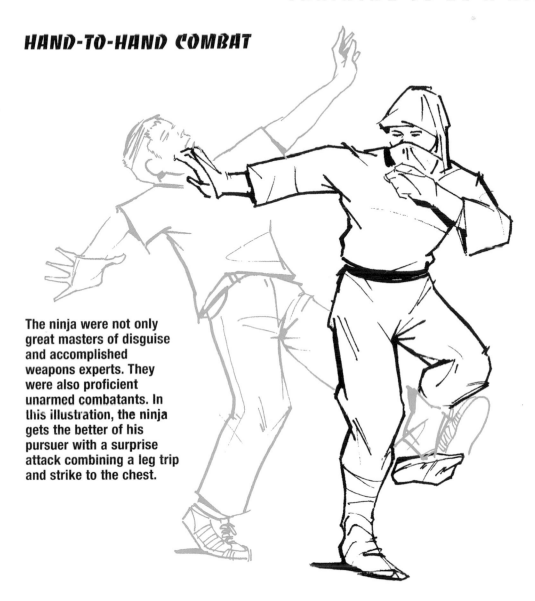

The ninja were not only great masters of disguise and accomplished weapons experts. They were also proficient unarmed combatants. In this illustration, the ninja gets the better of his pursuer with a surprise attack combining a leg trip and strike to the chest.

target in Japan's feudal culture. In other words, she is trained in the arts of seduction. If she is both attractive and a gifted musician, a female ninja agent (called a **kunoichi**) may pose as an entertainer or **courtesan** in order to get close to her victim. In this role, she will wear hair ornaments and carry musical instruments that contain hidden weapons and

NINJA WEAPONS

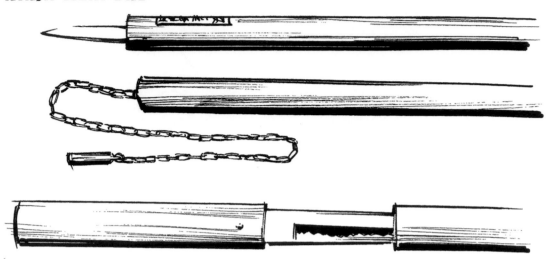

When infiltrating an enemy position in disguise, the ninja carried blade and chain weapons hidden in their staffs and walking sticks. Once safely inside a building, they were able to unleash their weapons at lightning speed before their target had a chance to react.

compartments for poisons. A kunoichi in a much more humble disguise, such as that of a maid or washerwoman, can also infiltrate an enemy stronghold more easily than her male colleagues.

Another vital part of ninjutsu training is in techniques of what we would now call "psychological warfare"; that is, attacking the enemy by playing on his or her mental weaknesses, such as laziness, fear, greed, or anger. The ninja classify these weaknesses according to the five elements: earth, air, fire, water, and wood, following old, established Chinese practices. The emotional anger that could be used to confuse an enemy was associated with the element fire. Lies and fabrications that led to internal dissension and suspicion in the enemy camp were linked to the element air. A favored ploy was to implicate an enemy leader's senior adviser and generals in some fabricated traitorous plot.

The enemy lord, fearing for his life, would unwittingly have his faithful servants executed. So, the planting of misleading information and the spreading of false rumors are also key weapons in the ninja's arsenal.

The final areas in which the ninja train are the techniques and rituals of Mikkyo (also known as Shugendo), an occult sect of Buddhism. At first sight, Mikkyo rituals appear to be a crude form of magic. The ninja makes signs in the air and joins his or her fingers in specific patterns to ward off evil and to call for supernatural aid on his or her mission. However, training in Mikkyo is more than just casting empty spells. In addition to their already fearsome reputation as fighters, the ninja are

A ninja springs a surprise attack from the banks of a river. The fighting staff he is holding is called a bo staff. These came in varying lengths, and were disguised as walking sticks when the ninja posed as a priest or traveling merchant.

also believed to possess occult powers. (In the superstitious 14th century, this served to further terrify their enemies.) Mikkyo also teaches the ninja other skills, such as meditation and breathing techniques. These techniques help the ninja to face danger in a calm manner.

HIRING A NINJA

Now fully trained, our young ninja siblings are ready to go into action. Naturally, they do not go and advertise their skills in the nearest town, and then wait until someone hires them. The ninja code is one of absolute secrecy. So how does a prospective employer contact the ninja? The ninja, like the samurai, are organized in a strict **hierarchy**. The ninja field agents are the genin, or the "low" men; their immediate superiors are the chunin, or the "middle" men; and the bosses, who decide which jobs to take, are the jonin, or the "high" men.

In Koga, as many as 50 chunin families control around 50 ninja genin each. But in Iga, three jonin families control up to 1,000 ninja genin each. If he does not have his own ninja training school, a feudal lord wishing to employ the services of a ninja clan cannot contact it directly. He has to send a representative to a province where they are known to operate, and then wait until they decide to make contact with him. This means of communication may seem absurd today, but in feudal Japan, when people did not travel much and strangers were immediately noticed, it was relatively easy for the chunin to make contact with their prospective clients. The chunin would then contact the jonin, who would decide whether or not to accept the mission. The jonin then instructed the chunin as to how many genin he would need to recruit for the mission. The genin never knew the identity of the

THE SAMURAI CODE OF HONOR

The highest virtue in the samurai honor code is loyalty to one's lord. This virtue is known as *bushido*. In the famous tale of the 47 ronin, the retainers of a murdered feudal lord stop at nothing until they have avenged his death and killed his murderer. To the samurai, the ninja, who lived and breathed treachery and deception, were the lowest of the low. Any ninja captured by a samurai could expect the most horrible of deaths. Ninja were trained to kill themselves rather than be captured. This later expanded to Japanese military personnel. The concept of seppuku, or ritual suicide, was even used during World War II, continuing the tradition of not surrendering.

client or of their ultimate jonin superior.

The process of hiring a ninja was perilous for many of the people concerned. The feudal lord could not be entirely sure that he was not hiring a ninja who might have a grudge against him. He also could not be sure that he was not being double-crossed by a jonin also working for one of his rivals. To ensure the loyalty of the ninja he had hired, a feudal lord might set tests or hire other ninja to observe them. Likewise, the chunin and genin also had to watch their backs, as they themselves might be considered "expendable" by the jonin, who might be willing to sacrifice them as mere pawns in a larger game.

Although they were masters of deceit, the ninja also had their own honor code. They did not follow the samurai's rigid bushido, but, in their own way, the ninja were fiercely loyal to family and clan. Although

These two ninja fighters combine swordsmanship and unarmed combat. While disarming his attacker, the man on the left prepares to deliver a hand strike to the chest.

later in their history, they were little better than common bandits, in their heyday, they were first and foremost superbly trained professional men and women whose sole concerns were duty to their clan and to the success of their missions.

THE FLYING NINJA

One of Japan's most famous ninja was called Sarutobi Sasuke. Sarutobi means "flying monkey," a nickname which he earned because of his almost superhuman ability to jump great distances. Sarutobi seemed to live a charmed life, but he, too, finally succumbed one day to the cunning of another ninja. Betrayed and discovered, he fled for his life across a garden, where his enemy had set mantraps. The unlucky Sarutobi stepped on one, but rather than be caught and tortured to death, he cut off his own foot to escape the trap. The shock of the injury, however, together with the loss of blood, was fatal to Sarutobi, who died soon after.

Weaponry and Tools

The ninja are perhaps best known for their weaponry. Because the ninja agent's aim was to infiltrate enemy territory, complete his or her mission, and escape without being detected, many of the weapons that he or she carried were designed to avoid a direct confrontation. Such weapons included those that could be used to kill or disable a guard or samurai from a distance.

The ninja was also equipped with weapons that gave him or her a longer reach than the fearsome samurai sword (the katana), weapons for close-quarter fighting, and composite weapons that could also be used as tools.

The ninja usually entered enemy territory in disguise, so the weapons he or she carried had to be undetectable. Like the gadgets designed for the famous spy character, James Bond, they should be easy to hide on the ninja's body or be disguised as harmless-looking objects and tools that he or she could carry without arousing suspicion. Furthermore, all weapons should be able to serve more than one purpose. The ninja

The secret of the ninja arsenal was not just that they used unusual or unique weapons, but also in the way they turned household tools, agricultural implements, and other innocent objects into weapons.

NINJUTSU

NINJA SWORDS

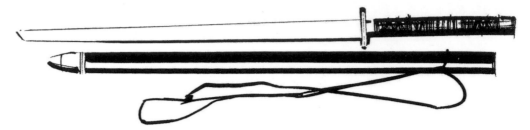

The ninjato, or ninja sword, is a much more practical and plain object than the highly decorated katana used by the samurai. It was also a multipurpose tool that could be used for digging and climbing.

arsenal contained hundreds of weapons; a single ninja agent could not hope to master all of them. Thus, the ninja, or his or her family, chose the weapons that he or she would specialize in.

The ninja's main opponent, the samurai warrior, was a superbly trained and well-armed fighting machine. The samurai recognized the ninja's effectiveness, and so they also trained themselves in the use of ninja weaponry in order to be able to counter the ninja effectively.

In those days, the average humble foot soldier or castle guard carried a halberd or spear as his weapon of choice, because the extra reach of these weapons was such that he did not need to be a skilled fighter in order to wound or kill an attacker. The samurai, however, wielded the katana. A warrior's katana was so precious that it was said to be his soul.

Japanese swords are admired as some of the finest in the world. The blades are forged from repeatedly hammered layers of steel, which gives the swords both incredible strength and flexibility. The finish on the sword, the **tsuba** (guard), and the scabbard were all of the highest quality, and were highly ornamented, with lacquer finishes and precious metal inlays. Before being handed to their owners, the best blades were tested on criminals—which no doubt would have included captured ninja agents.

Samurai trained from an early age in kenjutsu, the precursor of kendo and iaido, the two modern martial arts that are based on traditional swordplay techniques. An unarmed attacker faced with a katana wielded in expert hands had little or no chance of survival. The ninja also trained in kenjutsu, but only carried a katana when disguised as samurai. When infiltrating enemy territory, the ninja took along a very different sword: the ninjato.

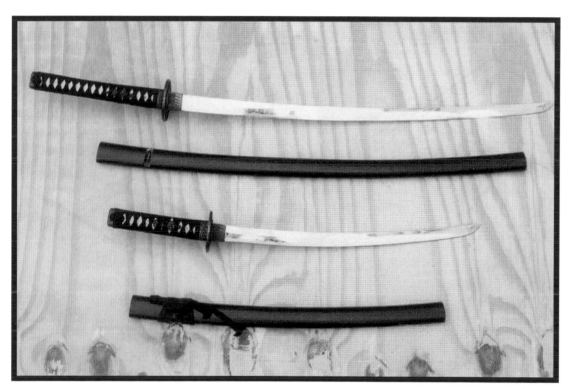

The samurai's main weapons were the katana, the long sword, and the short sword. The ninja, too, were trained in kenjutsu (swordplay), but they only carried the katana when they impersonated samurai.

NINJA SWORDS

The ninjato was not like the finely crafted, finished blade of the samurai. More like a long woodsman's knife or a machete, it was a much more serviceable and cheaply made item that could easily be replaced and discarded without a moment's thought. It had a shorter blade than the katana, which allowed it to be hidden when worn on a sash across the back. It could also be hidden under clothing. Even when worn over clothes, it was short enough not reveal the ninja's silhouette as that of an armed man or woman.

SWORD TECHNIQUES

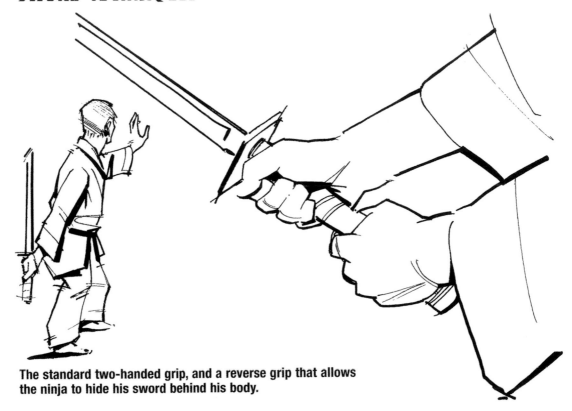

The standard two-handed grip, and a reverse grip that allows the ninja to hide his sword behind his body.

The ninjato's shorter reach meant that the ninja's fighting stance and attack style were different from those of classical kenjutsu techniques. The aim of ninja swordsmanship was not to demonstrate fine swash-buckling technique in a one-to-one duel with a samurai; rather, it was to knock out an opponent before he or she even had a chance to draw his or her own sword. Ninja sword training emphasized both the quick-draw and the surprise attack.

The standard sword grip for both the katana and ninjato is with the right hand just below the guard and the left hand just above the pommel (the knob on the sword's hilt). The gap between the two hands gives added flexibility to the swordsman to change grips. However, the ninja also used unorthodox grips and sword techniques to outwit and surprise their samurai opponents. The reverse grip, for example, enabled the ninja to hide his or her sword from an opponent behind his or her body.

The ninjato had several other uses, as well as several other designs to accommodate these uses. For example, the scabbards of some ninjato were made longer than the blades. This design allowed for a secret compartment at the end of the scabbard that could store poisons or powders. Scabbards could also be used as blowpipes, clubs, and snorkels for underwater swimming, or as levers to pry doors and windows open. The tsuba on the ninjato was larger than the one on the traditional katana, and could be used as a makeshift stepping platform when climbing over an obstacle. The long cord attached to the scabbard allowed the ninja to haul up his or her sword after climbing, and could also be used to strangle or restrain a guard.

SHURIKEN-THROWING BLADES

Shuriken come in two basic shapes: single-pointed blades shaped like knives, and multipointed "throwing stars" with between three and eight points.

LONG-RANGE WEAPONRY

The ninja's trademark weapon was undoubtedly the shuriken, the throwing blade or star. Shuriken came in a variety of shapes and sizes: with spike-like blades or with multipointed blades that had between three and eight points. A ninja carried nine shuriken, a number considered lucky (possibly because kyu, which means "nine" in Japanese, also means "suffering"). Their throwing range was limited to about 30 feet (10 m). They could also be used in close-quarter fighting as makeshift blades.

The spiked shuriken was the most effective of the two designs. It could actually kill an adversary—its single point was capable of causing a

THROWING THE SHURIKEN

Grasp the shuriken by one of its points, holding it horizontal to the ground.

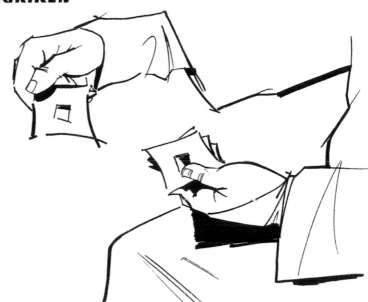

Use a snapping motion of the wrist and forearm to launch the shuriken.

deep wound. In contrast, the multipointed shuriken, although requiring less skill to use, did not penetrate as deeply, and thus could only injure. Nevertheless, a well-aimed shuriken, fired at the hands or face, could disable a warrior.

Shuriken were also multipurpose tools. A wafer-thin shuriken with a central hole could be thrown to make a whistling sound that could act as a decoy for a ninja infiltrating an enemy position. They could

BLOWPIPES

The ninja blowpipe could be used to kill with a poisoned dart, or to blow blinding powders into the eyes of guards or explosives into fires to cause diversions.

GUNPOWDER

Gunpowder was invented in China, but the Chinese did not develop firearms. However, their knowledge of fireworks came to Japan long before it was learned of in the West. The resourceful ninja made primitive hand grenades from hollowed-out eggs, simple mortars, and even land mines. These weapons were used against groups of opponents, or as decoys.

also serve as makeshift tools and could be used to pry open doors and windows and remove nails.

The star shuriken was grasped by one of the points and thrown horizontally, using a snapping motion in the wrist and forearm, with the wrist held straight. The ninja trained so that they could launch their shuriken with little or no body movement, to avoid detection.

A closely related weapon to the shuriken is the testubishi, a diamond or pyramid shape made of solid metal or intertwined metal spikes. This weapon was sometimes thrown like a shuriken, but was more often scattered in the path of a pursuer. As the Japanese do not wear shoes inside their houses, these devices were particularly effective in slowing down an enemy in pursuit.

Another favorite long-range weapon of the ninja was the blowpipe, which could fire poisoned darts and needles. It could also fire metsubushi, blinding powders made of ashes and containing irritants, such as chili pepper, that were blown in the eyes of enemies. Some ninja even trained in the dangerous art of blowing poisoned needles out of their mouths. The ninja long-range arsenal also contained explosive devices.

The weapons shown here—from left to right, the kama, tonfa, and nunchaku—were adapted from East Asian agricultural implements. The samurai, too, trained in their use once they realized that the ninja were using them.

When faced by a katana-wielding samurai, the ninja had other options to fall back on besides his or her shorter, inferior ninjato. A ninja disguised as a Buddhist priest, pilgrim, or traveling merchant carried a bo, a traditional hardwood fighting staff. The staff came in three lengths: approximately three feet (1 m), four feet (1.3 m), and six feet (1.8 m). The art of fighting using a staff is called bojutsu.

Both ninja and samurai in feudal Japan practiced bojutsu. The advantage of the staff is that, in expert hands, its increased reach made it an effective weapon against as many as five armed opponents. The ninja also carried hollow staffs known as shinobizue, which contained a length of chain. These staffs could be used to subdue an opponent by snagging his or her sword or arm. Bo and walking sticks could also hide blades.

Ninja fighters learned to coordinate their attacks with the bo with their body movements—thereby increasing the power behind the blows—and to hit with the tip of the staff rather than its length. Fighting moves included pole-vaulting with the staff, a technique that could also be employed to jump over obstacles.

Two other long-reach weapons employed by the ninja were the **kusarigama** and the kyoketsu shoge. The samurai also used the kusarigama, but the ninja version was smaller and more easily concealed. This weapon consisted of a **sickle** on a wooden handle attached to a length of chain, with a weight at the other end. As well as being used to cut and slash, the kusarigama could counter a sword blow, or be used to ensnare an enemy's blade or arm. The chain could

FIGHTING STAFF

The bo, or fighting staff, was a common weapon of the samurai as well as the ninja. The ninja, however, often hid weapons in hollow staffs.

also be used as a flail to injure opponents or keep them at bay.

A similar weapon, the kyoketsu shoge, consisted of a small hand sickle with an extra spur blade sticking out of the base of the main blade.

Instead of a chain and weight, the kyoketsu shoge had a 12-foot (4-m) cord made from woven animal or human hair with a large metal ring attached to the other end. A typical technique was for the ninja to throw the ring at his or her opponent. If the intended victim were foolish enough to catch the ring, the ninja would flick the rope and loop it around the victim's wrist. The kyoketsu shoge was also used as a tool, and its rope was also used as a climbing aid.

CLOSE-QUARTER WEAPONRY

Even apparently unarmed, the ninja could be lethal at close quarters. Easily hidden was the **kusarifundo**, a short length of chain with

CHAIN WEAPONS

The kusarifundo was a short length of chain weighted at each end. It could be used to snag an opponent's hand or sword.

The kusarigama was a sickle attached to a length of chain with a weight at the end.

Ninja were not only taught to fight in the controlled environment of the dojo, but also in situations closely resembling the conditions they would encounter in the field.

weights on either end. The ninja used this weapon to stop or snare an opponent's katana or arm, or to strangle him or her.

Although the ninja hardened their hands so as to be able to deliver knock-out punches, when they were faced with armor (which would protect the wearer from blows), the ninja wore the cat's claw, a glove-

CLIMBING TOOLS

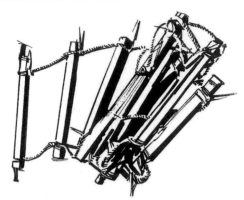 

The rope ladder (left) and kanigawa, or grappling iron (right) were the ninja's most popular tools for scaling castle walls. Both reduced to a manageable size and were easy to carry.

like device made of leather and metal that the ninja could rake across his or her opponent's flesh or use to pierce his or her armor. The shuko, an iron claw, was another good climbing tool, and could also be used to stop and hold a sword blade or to injure an attacker.

NINJA TOOLS AND HOUSES

Japanese castles were built in tiers: a broad base supported by progressively narrower stages. The commanding general or feudal lord usually took up residence in the uppermost levels, which had the best view of any approaching force, and was thus considered the safest from enemy attack.

To get into a castle, the first obstacle the ninja had to cross was the moat. He or she would swim under the moat using a snorkel, or would float across it on an inflatable device. Once inside the outer fortifications, the ninja would use his or her kanigawa, a 30-foot (10-m) length of rope with a grappling iron at one end, as well as rope ladders, to scale the walls.

Although the kanigawa was primarily a climbing tool, it could also be used to flail at the enemy or to ensnare him or her. The seemingly impregnable Japanese castle was, in fact, full of openings through which a ninja could enter. Once inside, the ninja could hide under the floor or behind a false ceiling.

Few ninja houses have survived the centuries, but there are a number of them still in Western Japan, including one in Kyoto, which is open to tourists. An unassuming merchant's house, it is full of secret compartments to hide weapons and documents, secret passageways, ladders, tunnels, and floors with built-in squeaks to alert the occupants to the presence of intruders. It is an intriguing insight into the history of the ninja and how these warriors used to live.

THE INTRODUCTION OF THE GUN

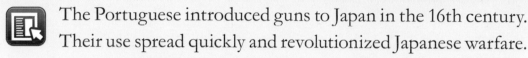 The Portuguese introduced guns to Japan in the 16th century. Their use spread quickly and revolutionized Japanese warfare. The gun was a deadly weapon, even in relatively untrained hands. Worst of all, it could be used to kill at a distance. A guard could pick off an approaching ninja a long time before he or she came into the range of the ninja's own long-range weapons. Likewise, an assassin not trained in ninjutsu could murder a general or feudal lord without even coming close to his or her victim. Not surprisingly, the long-term effect of the introduction of guns was to devalue both the unarmed and armed fighting skills of the samurai and ninja.

WORDS TO UNDERSTAND

wa Intention; subtle signs in posture and body language indicating what a person intends to do before he or she actually initiates the action

Unarmed Fighting Techniques

The ninja's strong point was the use of weapons. If he or she were dis-armed, however, he or she could always fall back on his or her training in taijutsu. Translated literally as "body art," this art was commonly known as "the art of unarmed combat."

Tutored in a combination of Japanese and Chinese unarmed fighting techniques, the ninja was a formidable opponent, even against an armed guard. Like the ninja weapons' techniques, the aim of taijutsu was not to engage in an honorable and time-consuming duel with an opponent, but to disable or kill him or her before he or she had a chance to react. In ninja fighting, there were no rules: only winning and losing.

As we have seen, one of the theories for the origins of ninjutsu was that the Iga and Koga ninja clans had been taught their skills by Chinese exiles and Japanese monks (these monks had visited China to bring back the holy texts of the Buddhist religion). The links between Buddhism and the martial arts in China date back to the 6th century A.D., when the Indian monk Bodhidharma (A.D. 470–534) made the perilous three-year overland journey from India to China to teach a

Taijutsu, the ninja's unarmed fighting techniques, owes a great deal to Chinese kung fu, the techniques of which were brought to Japan by Chinese exiles and Japanese Buddhist monks.

The descendants of the original Shaolin kung fu monks continue to practice and spread the tactics developed by long-ago disciples.

new form of Buddhism called Dhyana. One day, Dhyana would become Zen Buddhism in Japan.

After an unsuccessful meeting with the Emperor Wu, who could not understand Bodhidharma's teachings, the monk retired to a monastery at the foot of Songshan Mountain in Honan Province. The monastery's name, which would one day become important in the annals of kung fu, was Shaolin.

The monks of the Shaolin monastery were devout and strong in spirit, but they were weak of body. Bodhidharma found they did not have the strength or stamina to withstand the long hours of meditation that his teachings required. To remedy this situation, he taught the monks a set of 18 movements to improve their health and

NATURAL STANCE

The ninja had to be ready to fight at all times, but he could not give his hostile intent away. In the natural stance, he feigns relaxation while being alert and ready to strike.

fitness. Over the centuries, these exercises were refined and expanded, and developed into the Shaolin lohan kung fu fighting method. This method is the basis for many of present-day China's unarmed fighting techniques.

Through direct teaching from Chinese visitors or indirect teachings from Japanese monks and yamabushi warrior-ascetics (it is not known which), the ninja families had knowledge of Chinese kung fu techniques. The ninja blended these techniques with Japan's own ancient fighting systems: sumo wrestling and jujutsu. They created their own hybrid fighting style, which they called taijutsu. Taijutsu was divided into two types of techniques: dakentaijutsu (striking techniques) and jutaijutsu (grappling techniques).

STANCE AND APPROACH

As in all martial arts training, the first techniques the ninja learned were the stances of their art. Stance determines a person's balance, striking range, and how much of a target he or she will present to the enemy. In martial arts such as karate, the fighting stances are strong and deep, which makes them immediately apparent. A ninja, however, had to be prepared to fight at a moment's notice, but yet had to appear relaxed, with his or her stance natural, so as not to draw attention to him- or herself or give him- or herself away. One important stance was called the shizen no kamae (the natural stance).

Training in stances begins simply with adopting and holding each stance in turn. This can be more challenging than it appears, however, especially if you are holding a very low stance.

HORSE STANCE

The horse stance builds muscular strength and endurance in the legs. Here, a training ninja is in a wide receiving stance, ready to face multiple attackers in a seemingly undefendable pose.

ATTACK STANCE

This is also known as the front stance. The weight is distributed 60:40 over the front and rear feet.

HORSE STANCE

The most basic martial arts stance after shizen no kamae is the double-weighted kiba dachi (horse stance).

In this stance, the weight was distributed on both legs, which were spread wider than hip-width distance apart. Standing in kiba dachi, the student ninja had to learn to repel attacks from any direction—and from more than one assailant.

FORWARD, OR ATTACK, STANCE

In this stance, the ninja's feet are hip-width apart, with about 60 percent of his or her weight on his or her front foot. His or her hands were raised, to guard from attack to the body and face.

From this position, the ninja could face his or her opponent squarely or with his or her body turned at a 45-degree angle to reduce the striking area. This stance provided an extremely stable foundation from which to strike with either the hand or foot.

REAR, OR DEFENSIVE, STANCE

This stance required the ninja to shift 60 to 70 percent of his or her weight onto his or her rear foot, with both feet on the same line. His or her torso was angled, so as to present a smaller target to his or her opponent. The ninja's arms were positioned to protect the centerline of his or her body and face. In addition to stability, the rear stance allowed the ninja to avoid an opponent's attacks without having to change his or her footing. It also provided a good starting point for a kicking attack.

STANCES AND CHI

Shizen no kamae (the natural stance) is not a specific stance (like the other three described), but more of a state of mind. In

DEFENSIVE STANCE

This is also known as the rear stance. The weight is distributed 70:30 over the rear and front feet.

63

A modern-day ninja, clothed all in black, produces a flying attack on an imaginary enemy during training. Because the ninja were so adept at moving undetected, they could conduct these attacks with ease.

the natural stance, the ninja had to combine complete readiness with the difficult art of masking his or her **wa** (intention). In addition to obvious things like stance, posture, and hand position, this also meant controlling his or her body language, as well as the subtle energy that the Chinese call chi.

The ancient Chinese believed that chi was the energy that bound the universe together and animated all living things. Chi flows through our

HIDDEN COUNTERATTACK

After blocking the attacker's punch, the ninja counters with a kick to the chest. The element of surprise was vital to the ninja.

NINJA HAND WEAPONS

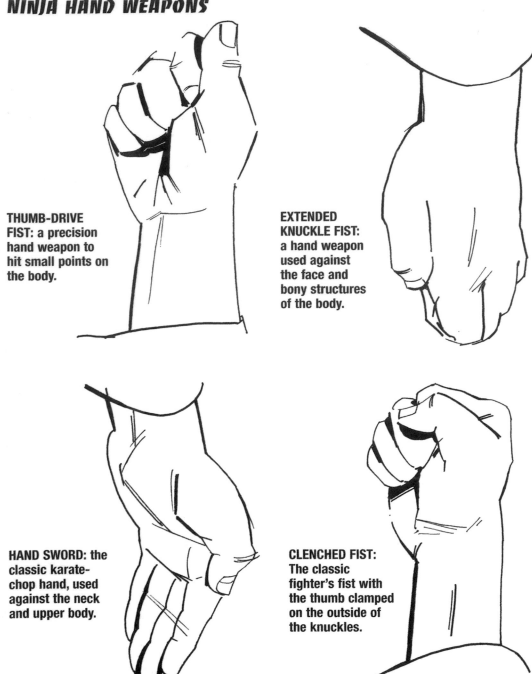

THUMB-DRIVE FIST: a precision hand weapon to hit small points on the body.

EXTENDED KNUCKLE FIST: a hand weapon used against the face and bony structures of the body.

HAND SWORD: the classic karate-chop hand, used against the neck and upper body.

CLENCHED FIST: The classic fighter's fist with the thumb clamped on the outside of the knuckles.

bodies via an invisible network of channels called meridians. (Chinese doctors insert needles into meridians when they are treating patients with acupuncture.) Chi does not only animate the mechanical functions of the body, such as breathing and blood circulation; it can also reveal a person's wa.

An advanced martial artist trained in an internal art such as t'ai chi ch'uan (supreme ultimate fist) can freely direct his or her own chi, and also sense the chi of others. During his or her spiritual training in Mikkyo Buddhism, the ninja learned techniques such as meditation and breathing exercises that allowed him or her to disguise both his or her chi and wa.

In an attack situation, the ninja had to mask his or her approach, and used many techniques to enter, act, and depart unseen. Even when fighting unarmed, the ninja used deception and surprise to overcome his or her opponent. Instead of coming at his or her enemy head-on, like a Western boxer would, the ninja's approach was oblique. The ninja might pretend to flee, and then suddenly turn to strike his or her now overconfident pursuer. Or, he or she might appear to strike an obvious target with one hand (that the opponent would easily spot and parry), while dealing out a killing blow at an unforeseen target with the other.

DEADLY WEAPONS

A ninja on a mission would carry a fearsome array of objects and tools that could be used as weapons. Even if he or she was disarmed, however, the ninja still had an arsenal of weapons at his or her disposal: his or her hands, feet, elbows, knees, and head. The hand was the most versatile of these bodily weapons, as it could be formed into a variety of different

COMBINATION ATTACK

STEP 1: A single blow will rarely finish an opponent, especially one trained in the martial arts. The ninja used a series of linked attacks for specific targets to disable or kill an opponent quickly.

STEP 2: Having avoided his opponent's attack by sidestepping inside his attacking fist, the ninja struck his opponent's face with a straight punch, with his fist in fudoken.

weapons. These included the fudoken (clenched fist), shikanken (extended-knuckle fist), shuto (hand sword), and the boshiken (thumb-drive fist).

The fudoken is the standard clenched fist, with the fingers curled into the palm and the thumb clamped on the outside. The striking surface is the knuckles. This type of fist could be used against any part of the body. The more specialized ninja fists included the shikanken, which was used against the face and bony structures, and the boshiken, which was used against semi-soft targets and specific weak points. The shuto, although not a fist, was an angled "karate-chop" hand that was used against the neck and to smash the limbs. In addition to his or her hands, the ninja excelled at using any part of the body to strike an opponent, which he or she hid with low, oblique movements and feints. The ninja had the ability to hide his body, his weapons, and his intention to strike.

STEP 3: He immediately followed up his punch with an elbow strike to his opponent's ear or temple. As he struck with his elbow, he folded the other hand into either the fudoken or shikanken, to continue his attack.

STEP 4: A final strike to a pressure point on the face completed the attack.

UNARMED COMBAT TECHNIQUES

The following techniques are meant only to give a flavor of the ninja unarmed fighting style and are not comprehensive. They are, however, real techniques, and should be treated with caution. Make sure that you and your prospective partner have warmed up and stretched your joints and muscles before attempting the throws. Practice the striking techniques on an inanimate target, such as a punching bag or a dummy. Always remember that the martial arts can be dangerous.

COMBINATION MOVES

Ninja had to be ready to attack or defend themselves from any position. A ninja would escape from an attacker by squatting, and would then use his or her hands and feet together to strike in retaliation. Striking the upper body (face or chest) with the heel of his or her hand, he or she would hook his or her opponent's leg and pull forward with his or her foot. Once the opponent was on the ground, it was only a matter of finishing him or her off.

HIDDEN COUNTERATTACKS

Standing in a wide stance, facing sideways to his or her attacker with the right foot leading, the ninja neutralized his or her opponent's attacking punch. He or she would then jump, turning his or her body 360 degrees, and kick the opponent in the chest or stomach with the left foot.

LOW SWEEP

In this low-leg sweep, the ninja dives to the ground to avoid his opponent's kick and responds with a sweep to overbalance him.

SWEEP

Martial arts such as judo and jujutsu specialize in closing in on an attacker, taking him or her down with a throw, and then finishing him or her off with a blow, strangle, or arm lock.

In this classic sweep, the ninja stepped past the opponent's attacking arm, then grasped the opponent's neck and right arm, stepped around with his or her right leg, lowered his or her hips, and thrust them back into him or her, pulling the opponent over. The ninja never let go of a thrown opponent, as he or she might roll out of the fall and make a counterattack, and always followed up his or her advantage with a killing strike.

LOW-LEG SWEEP

Having avoided an opponent's kick by dropping to the floor, the ninja rested his or her body weight on his or her hands as he or she swung his or her leg around, literally sweeping his or her opponent's leg out from underneath him or her.

CLASSIC SWEEP

Pulling his opponent off balance, the ninja steps around his opponent and sweeps his supporting leg from under him.

THE ART OF INVISIBILITY

Above all, the ninja worked in the shadows. If they were discovered and had to fight their way out, their mission was deemed a partial failure. The successful ninja "hit" was one that no one was aware of until the ninja had returned safely to his or her base.

The ninja employed many "invisibility" techniques to avoid detection when infiltrating enemy territory and to escape from pursuers if they were discovered. This, of course, does not mean that the ninja literally made themselves invisible. Although there were many tales about the ninja's supernatural abilities to vanish or change shape at will and to leap huge distances with a single bound, Superman-style, these tales were spread by the ninja themselves to awe and frighten their enemies.

Ninja "invisibility" consisted of some practical techniques—some extremely simple, others much more complex—that deceived the senses of sight, hearing, smell, taste, and touch. The ninja knew that sight was the human being's dominant sense, that it had a much greater range than the other four, and that it was the hardest to fool.

Three factors determine a human's ability to see an object: its color,

The ninja employed many techniques, some simple and some complex, to become "invisible" to their enemies. Here, a ninja uses handy vegetation to escape discovery.

NINJUTSU

INFILTRATION

Climbing unseen into an enemy stronghold was one of the most important skills of the ninja. They carried a variety of climbing aids, and also had incredible stamina to hang immobile for many hours.

its shape, and whether or not it is moving. The first technique that the ninja learned in order to avoid being seen was how to become completely still. This may seem obvious, but it is actually extremely difficult to maintain perfect stillness, especially if you are crouching in an uncomfortable position or hanging from a rope on the outside of a building. Because the eye is drawn to movement, a classic ploy of the ninja was to throw an object to distract the guards, which gave the ninja enough time to reach the objective. The ninja also trained in meditation techniques, drawn from both Mikkyo and Zen Buddhism, which allowed them to remain immobile for long periods of time.

Terrain and vegetation could be used in different ways to hide the ninja's approach. Apart from hiding in this long grass, the ninja would also set fire to it to cause confusion or mask an escape.

Once a guard spotted movement, he would try to identify the object by its shape or silhouette. A man standing or running has a distinctive silhouette, with a head, two arms, and two legs. The ninja distorted their silhouettes by changing the shape of their bodies, drawing in their limbs and lowering their heads. They would also hold up a scarf or jacket in front of themselves to alter their outline.

The third and final factor determining whether or not we see something is its color. The ninja agent's costume consisted of loose-fitting pants, a jacket, a hood or scarf, and footwear. All of these items were black, which made them almost impossible to see at night. The jacket was lined with a colored fabric so that if it were reversed in the daylight, the ninja could lose him- or herself in a crowd.

The various ninja families and schools had their own closely guarded invisibility techniques, but they also had many methods in common. These were divided into different classes of techniques: elementals, the heavens, living creatures, and manmade objects.

ELEMENTALS

The Japanese, along with the Chinese, recognized five cosmic elements, adding the element of wood to the classic elements of fire, water, air, and earth.

FIRE

Paradoxically, fire and light could be used by the ninja to avoid detection in several ways. Open fires and braziers (pans containing burning coals) were used for lighting and warmth in all buildings in feudal Japan. A

Left: The ninja often chose to approach an enemy stronghold by the most difficult and arduous route, which would also be the least well guarded, and catch the enemy by surprise.

NINJUTSU

FIRE ELEMENTS

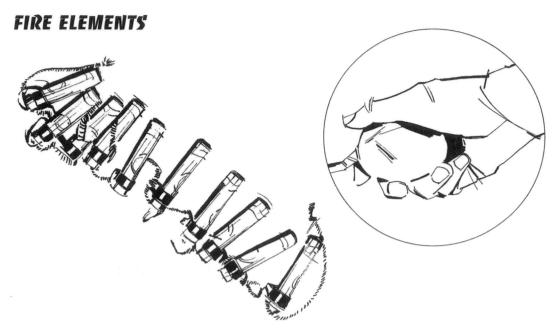

MAIN IMAGE: A string of firecrackers could be thrown into a fire to create panic in the enemy camp and allow a ninja to enter or leave undiscovered.
INSET: The ninja used primitive guns as well as explosive charges, such as this grenade, to attack and also to distract their enemies.

favored ploy of a ninja attempting to infiltrate an enemy position was to throw a powder or special stone that would make a loud noise when heated in a fire to distract the guards' attention.

Similarly, light, which could give a ninja away, could also be turned to his or her advantage. For example, a sudden bright light in the darkness could be used to blind a guard just long enough to get past him. Other devices that involved fire included primitive explosives and firecrackers; these were thrown to mask the ninja's entry and escape, and to create panic. Ninja also set fires in vegetation, such as long grass, to confuse their enemies and to hide their own movements.

WATER

Traditional Japanese castle architecture and garden design made considerable use of bodies of water. Japanese castles were surrounded by one or more moats. While these moats provided a useful defense against an attacking army, they made the ninja's approach much more difficult to detect. Trained from a young age to swim, the ninja could easily cross a moat by swimming underwater with the aid of a snorkel, or on the surface with an inflatable flotation device. Japanese gardens, especially those of castles or daimyo mansions, had rivers, ponds, and ornamental lakes. These were ideal hiding places for a ninja, both before he or she made his or her "hit" and immediately afterwards, while he or she waited for things to calm down before escaping.

AIR

If natural fog or mist were not present, the ninja could mask his or her entrance and exit with a smoke bomb. Some ninja employed the theatrical "puff of smoke" as they disappeared into a tunnel or climbed a rope ladder to evade their pursuers, who would be mystified as to the

THE DRAGON BOAT

Legend has it that the ninja created the worlds first submersible warship, called the dragon boat, the only visible part of which was the dragon-shaped prow sticking out of the water. The dragon boat was used to infiltrate enemy territory by sea and to attack enemy boats. The dragon boat had no means of storing or renewing its oxygen supply, however, so its use was limited.

NINJUTSU

CLIMBING WITH THE SHUKO

The shuko, or iron claw, was made of iron spikes mounted onto leather straps. It was used by the ninja to climb Japan's wooden buildings as well as trees. It could also be used as a weapon in close-quarter fighting.

ninja's whereabouts when the smoke cleared.

The ninja also used various irritant powders that could be blown into a guard's face to blind him, as well as to check whether a person was really asleep—or merely pretending to sleep.

Other uses of the air included primitive gliders, which could carry a ninja into enemy territory, and giant kites. Attempts were made to fly a man on a large kite for reconnaissance and aerial warfare purposes, but these attempts were not successful. Kites with ninja painted on them, however, were flown to unsettle the enemy and were also used as decoys.

EARTH

The element earth had several meanings for the ninja. First, there was the lay of the land itself. Which features— cliffs, hills, or mountains—could he or she use to mask his or her approach? The ninja often came by routes that their enemies had left unguarded because they were considered impassable. Furthermore, the earth itself could provide sanctuary in the form of tunnels dug to enter or

SMALL STEP

To walk silently through waterlogged ground or low vegetation or fallen leaves, the weight is shifted onto one foot and the other lifted vertically, toes pointing down.

SIDE STEP

To walk through narrow spaces, such as between houses, or through a dense forested area, the ninja would move in a sideways manner, sliding one foot across and crossing over the other foot.

escape after a mission or in the form of hiding holes.

The element earth was also meaningful to the ninja in that it referred to the ninja's own position on the earth or his or her mode of moving. The ninja developed many different types of **ashi** (walks or steps), including ko ashi (small walk), yoko ashi (sideways walk), nuki ashi (stealthy or sweeping walk), suri ashi (rubbing walk), tobi ashi (flying walk), and so ashi (large walk). These movements were developed to help the ninja avoid detection on various kinds of terrain or when they were inside a building.

Ko ashi was used when walking through marshy ground or through dry vegetation, such as fallen leaves, when a normal method of walking would make a great deal of noise. The ninja kept his or her weight on one foot, then put the other foot down, toes pointed, passing smoothly through the surface and making little or no noise or disturbance. He or she then shifted his or her weight onto this foot, and then lifted his or her rear foot.

EMPTY STEP

When walking into an unlit building, which might have booby-trapped floors and trip wires, the ninja moved with great care. He would keep his weight on one foot and feel his way forward with the other.

The crab-like yoke ashi was useful in narrow passageways between and inside buildings and in densely planted bamboo groves and forests, where a party of pursuers with their swords drawn would soon become hopelessly entangled. In this walk, the ninja bent his or her knees deeply and crossed his or her feet.

Nuki ashi came into its own inside a building. Traditional Japanese houses have planking floors in the halls and corridor, and straw **tatami** mats in the living areas. In this walk, the ninja stayed low, with his or her weight on one leg. He or she would use the leading leg delicately, feeling for obstacles in his or her path, such as trip wires that were often placed there to detect intruders.

WOOD

During the feudal period, most of Japan was mountainous and thickly forested. This made it easy for the ninja to travel undetected. In open-warfare situations, or when waiting in ambush, vegetation provided the ideal camouflage, which the ninja improved upon by attaching plant matter to their clothing. In temples, mansions, and castles, large gardens and thick bamboo groves were common features. These provided ideal cover for the ninja, and also a means of escape, should he or she be discovered and pursued. The ninja also used trees as platforms for reconnaissance, climbing them with the assistance of the shuko claw.

Right: Trees provided natural camouflage for the ninja, and could be used to reconnoiter enemy positions from a safe distance. They also offered ideal entrance and escape routes from the gardens of mansions and castles.

THE SHUKO

The shuko, or iron claw, was a versatile device that could be used in fighting to grab an opponent's sword without injury to the hand.

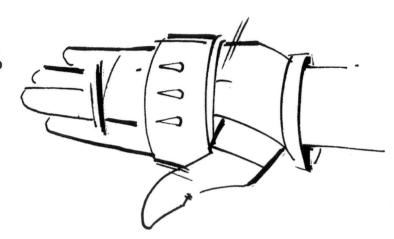

THE HEAVENS

The second class of ninja invisibility techniques used natural phenomena. The weather provided fog, mist, rain, snow, thunder, and lightning, with which a ninja could mask his or her approach. Even the sun and moon had their uses: a ninja approaching an enemy with the sun behind him or her would likely not be seen immediately.

LIVING CREATURES

The ninja used both humans and animals in their operations. Innocent bystanders could be used as decoys and covers for the ninja's activities. One more face in a crowd, the ninja could approach his or her target without attracting undue attention.

The ninja was also trained to disguise him- or herself when he or she needed to infiltrate enemy territory in daylight. The disguise a ninja chose suited his or her age and appearance. There were seven traditional disguises, known as the shichihode: yamabushi (mountain warrior-ascetic), sarugaku (entertainer), komuso (traveling priest), ronin (masterless samurai), akindo (merchant), hokashi (minstrel), and shukke (monk). The ninja not only had to take on the appearance of these roles, but also their movements and speech patterns if he or she were not to be unmasked. The ninja also trained animals, such as monkeys and dogs, to act as decoys and to attack pursuers.

MANMADE OBJECTS

This class of invisibility technique covered the use of any manmade object or structure. Traditional Japanese buildings, with their high roofs held up by wooden joinery and their raised floors and false ceilings, all provided a multitude of hiding places for the ninja. Other manmade objects that the ninja imitated were statues and scarecrows.

CAT'S CLAW

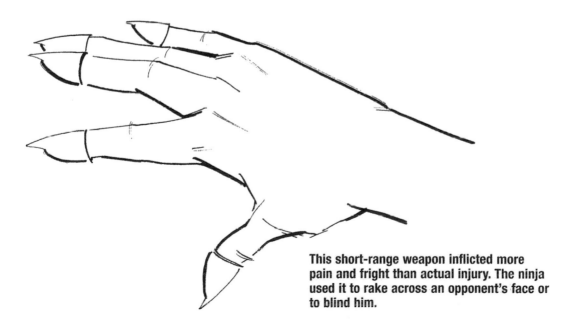

This short-range weapon inflicted more pain and fright than actual injury. The ninja used it to rake across an opponent's face or to blind him.

RESOURCES

Organizations such as the British SAS, the U.S. Navy SEALs, and other world special forces units are the ninja of modern times. They train in many of the same arts as their distant medieval forebears: armed and unarmed fighting techniques (but with weapons the ninja could only dream about), psychological warfare, and their own version of the "art of invisibility," which is close to true invisibility now with "stealth" technology.

The modern-day followers of ninjutsu, however, no longer sell their deadly services to the highest bidder. The modern schools of ninjutsu and nimpo that have opened in Japan and other parts of the world in the past decades combine the teaching of the martial arts, training in the use of ancient weaponry, and the re-creation of ancient costumes and lifestyles.

As in the other martial arts, there is a stress on self-discipline and fortitude in the face of adversity. Ninjutsu is not a game to be played with exotic weapons and outlandish costumes, but a spiritual path that can bring its students to a profound understanding of themselves and the world around them.

Right: A modern-day ninja begins to scale a wall in the manner of his forebears. All over the world, the sons and daughters of 21st-century workers and businesspeople are keeping the traditions of feudal Japan alive.

Glossary

Alliance   A joining together of individuals or groups to fight for a common cause

Ascetic   Someone who practices strict self-denial as a means of self-discipline

Ashi   Foot or leg; stepping techniques used in ninjutsu to camouflage an approach

Courtesan   A female courtier or prostitute

Daimyo   Semi-independent feudal lords who ruled the Japanese provinces from 1185 to 1867

Exile   Expulsion from a person's native country

Feudal   A social and political system in which peasants work for a powerful landowner in exchange for food and protection

Fiefdom   A piece of land held under the feudal system

Halberd   A combined spear and battle-ax

Hierarchy   A system in which grades of status or authority are ranked above each other

Kana   Any of various Japanese syllabic alphabets

Kanji   Chinese characters; the Japanese writing system uses three elements: kanji, which are pictograms that represent an entire word, and two syllabic alphabets, kana, to write word endings and foreign loan words

Kunoichi   Female ninja agent trained in the same arts and techniques as her male counterparts

Kusarifundo	Short length of chain with weights on either end used in close-quarter combat
Kusarigama	Sickle on a wooden handle attached to a length of chain
Monarch	The ruler of a country
Paddy	A field where rice is grown
Ronin	Samurai warrior who has lost his master
Ruse	A lie; a trick
Shinto	Native religion of Japan, which stresses the holiness of natural objects that are believed to be the home of the kami, or gods
Sickle	Short-handled farming tool
Shogun	Military rulers of Japan from 1185 to 1867; several families held the title of shogun; the Tokugawa held it the longest, ruling for almost 270 years, from 1600 to 1867
Taijutsu	Literally, "body art," unarmed fighting techniques; these were based on Japan's own jujutsu (art of compliance) and martial arts techniques brought from China by Japanese Buddhist priests and Chinese exiles
Tatami	Injury-prevention mats made from woven rice straw
Tsuba	The guard on a Japanese sword that protects the handle from the blade
Wa	Intention; subtle signs in posture and body language indicating what a person intends to do before he or she actually initiates the action; this involves reading a person's chi

CLOTHING AND EQUIPMENT

CLOTHING

Gi: The gi is the most typical martial arts "uniform." Usually in white, but also available in other colors, it consists of a cotton thigh-length jacket and calf-length trousers. Gis come in three weights: light, medium, and heavy. Lightweight gis are cooler than heavyweight gis, but not as strong. The jacket is usually bound at the waist with a belt.

Belt: Belts are used in the martial arts to denote the rank and experience of the wearer. They are made from strong linen or cotton and wrap several times around the body before tying. Beginners usually wear a white belt, and the final belt is almost always black.

Hakama: A long folded skirt with five pleats at the front and one at the back. It is a traditional form of clothing in kendo, iaido, and jujutsu.

Zori: A simple pair of slip-on sandals worn in the dojo when not training to keep the floor clean.

WEAPONS

Bokken: A bokken is a long wooden sword made from Japanese oak. Bokken are roughly the same size and shape as a traditional Japanese sword (katana).

Jo: The jo is a simple wooden staff about 4–5 ft (1.3–1.6 m) long and is a traditional weapon of karate and aikido.

Kamma: Two short-handled sickles used as a fighting tool in some types of karate and jujutsu.

Tanto: A wooden knife used for training purposes.

Hojo jutsu: A long rope with a noose on one end used in jujutsu to restrain attackers.

Sai: Long, thin, and sharp spikes, held like knives and featuring wide, spiked handguards just above the handles.

Tonfa: Short poles featuring side handles, like modern-day police batons.

Katana: A traditional Japanese sword with a slightly curved blade and a single, razor-sharp cutting edge.

Butterfly knives: A pair of knives, each one with a wide blade. They are used mainly in kung fu.

Nunchaku: A flail-like weapon consisting of three short sections of staff connected by chains.

Shinai: A bamboo training sword used in the martial art of kendo.

Iaito: A stainless-steel training sword with a blunt blade used in the sword-based martial art of iaido.

FURTHER READING

Borda, Remiguisz and Marian Winecki. *The Illustrated Ninja Handbook.* New York: Tuttle Publishing, 2014.

Cummins, Antony and Yoshie Minami. *Iga and Koka Ninja Skills: The Secret Shinobi Scrolls of Chikamatsu Shinegori.* The History Press, 2013. *Note: The authors unearthed this centuries-old manuscript, which details the use of ninja techniques in Japan in the 1700s.*

Hatsumi, Masaaki. *The Complete Ninja: The Secret World Revealed.* New York: Kodansha USA, 2014. *Note: The author is a world-famous ninja grandmaster and ninja historian.*

SERIES CONSULTANT

Adam James is the Founder of Rainbow Warrior Martial Arts and the Director for the National College of Exercise Professionals. Adam is a 10th Level Instructor of Wei Kuen Do, Chi Fung, and Modern Escrima, and a 5th Degree Black Belt in Kempo, Karate, Juijitsu, and Kobudo. He is also the co-creator of the NCEP-Rainbow Warrior Martial Arts MMA Trainer certification program, which has been endorsed by the Commissioner of MMA for the State of Hawaii and by the U.S. Veterans Administration. Adam was also the Director of World Black Belt, whose Founding Members include Chuck Norris, Bob Wall, Gene LeBell, and 50 of the world's greatest martial artists. In addition, Adam is an actor, writer and filmmaker, and he has performed with Andy Garcia, Tommy Lee Jones, and Steven Seagal. As a writer, he has been published in numerous martial arts books and magazines, including *Black Belt*, *Masters Magazine*, and the *Journal of Asian Martial Arts*, and he has written several feature film screenplays.

Useful Web Sites

http://martialarts.org/

http://www.ninjutsu.com/

http://www. konigunninjutsu.com/

http://www.winjutsu.com/

http://www.ninjutsusociety.net/

Publisher's Note: The websites listed on this page were active at the time of publication. The publisher is not responsible for websites that have changed their address or discontinued operation since the date of publication. The publisher reviews and updates the websites each time the book is reprinted.

About the Author

Eric Chaline is a personal-training consultant and health and fitness journalist and author with credentials in the martial arts, Zen Buddhism, and yoga. After graduating from Cambridge University and the School of Oriental and African Studies in London, he studied in Japan at Osaka Foreign Studies University, where he pursued his interests in Japanese history, philosophy, and the martial arts. He remained in Japan after completing his studies and supervised the English-language martial arts publications of a major Japanese publisher, which included books on aikido by the current doshu, Ueshiba Morihei, and on kyudo, Japanese archery.

INDEX